Triple Citizenship

poems

Triple Citizenship

poems

by
Bruna Gomes

Encircle Publications, LLC
Farmington, Maine USA

Triple Citizenship ©2022 Bruna Gomes

Paperback ISBN-13: 978-1-64599-352-0
Kindle ISBN-13: 978-1-64599-353-7

All rights reserved. No part of this book may be reproduced in any form by any mechanical or electronic means including storage and retrieval systems without express written permission in writing from the publisher. Brief passages may be quoted in review. Rights to individual poems remain with the author.

Editor: Cynthia Brackett-Vincent
Book and book cover design: Eddie Vincent/ENC Graphics Services
Cover Image: Bruna Gomes

Sign up for Encircle Publications newsletter and specials
http://eepurl.com/cs8taP

Mail Orders, Author Inquiries:
Encircle Publications
PO Box 187
Farmington, ME USA 04938

Online orders:
encirclepub.com

for
my anchors
Vovó and Grandma

Contents

PART I

CITIZENSHIP TEST	3
MATADORS	5
BRASILEIRA	6
MAGICAL / REALISM	8
HOLDING HANDS WITH MY GRANDMOTHER	9
BITTER	10
GOING TO CHURCH	11
THE FIRST TIME I LEFT	13
SELF-PORTRAIT OF ME, A LANDSCAPE	14
OCEAN	15
in bed, thinking	16
insomniac says a prayer	17
ETYMOLOGY	18
PURITY (n)	19
CERAMIC CANOPIES	22
bossa nova	23
ROOM OF MIRRORS	24
LIMÃO	25
MILK AND OATS	26
LOVE	27
WHAT I KNOW	28
INCANTATION	29

PART II

AN OBSERVATION	33
that one time mary pranked us	34
AN ODE TO THE AUSTRALIAN SUMMER	35
RETROGRADE	37
LADY GAWAIN	38
PHOTO ALBUM	39
NOVEMBER	41
L90	42
GIFTS FROM YOU, BIG BLUE	43
FOOD CHAIN	45
SPRINGTIME	46

songs through text ... 47
MAURICE ... 48
PHARAOH ... 49
GROCER ... 50
ODE TO 12:30 AM ON A WEDNESDAY
(AND ITS SUCCESSOR, 8:15 AM) ... 51
A DINNER RESERVATION ... 52
THE DIVINE ESTATE ... 53
SECOND CHANCES ... 55
weeding is a hobby for the lonely ... 56
THE DREADED DINNER PARTY ... 57
DARLING, ... 58
anonymous ... 59

PART III

AN ORIGIN STORY ... 62
SÃO PAULO ... 63
WALKING / DEAD ... 64
THIEVES OF IGUAÇU ... 65
PRESERVED ... 67
SAINT DIVA ... 68
ANATOMY OF THE HAND OF VOVÓ ... 70
CENOURA E CEBOLA ... 71
POCKET-MAP ... 73
A 37-DEGREE DAY AT THE FEIRA ... 74
NECTAR ... 75
if the amazon rainforest is the lungs of the earth,
then somewhere in there is the heart ... 76
SYNONYMS FOR LIGHT ... 77
BRUNA ... 78
BRIGADEIRO RECIPE ... 80
HOW TO SAY "I LOVE YOU" ... 81
EVERYONE DIES ... 82
TESOURO ... 84
TUCANO IN THE SKY ... 86
GOMES ... 87
Acknowledgements ... 90
About the Author ... 91

PART I

*underwater labyrinth
urges current through borders*

CITIZENSHIP TEST

according to government papers
do i belong to the country that

      a) fights over me
      b) fights for me
      c) claims me as their best example

according to these pages
am i searching for the country

      a) in the flesh of their fruits
      b) in the twist of their tongues
      c) in the history of their soil
      d) none of the above. i am looking for myself.

i was told i could be

      a) a novelist
      b) a poet
      c) not both at the same time

if you answered (c)
apply the same rule to citizenships:

can i be

      a) australian on the phone to a friend
      b) brazilian at the dinner table
      c) american on my birth certificate

am i connected to

    a) what i am born with
    b) what i am born to become

consider the following passage:

    my roots span an
    entire universe, press me
    to a pulp and you'll see
    i am made of the seeds
    i haven't yet sown
    my branches reach
    to every / any
    resemblance of love

does the passage above tell me

    a) who i am
    b) where i am
    c) why i am

MATADORS

wannabe matadors
wave homemade capes
at beasts

hanging by horns
rag-doll roll across a soccer field
cleft hoof kick in the ribs and

die,
never

for a homemade man makes
a homemade living.

BRASILEIRA

half of me lives
on the other side of the globe
in a plate of papaya,
a kitchen
knife lodged into my shoulder,
as i get older
my grandmother's withered
hand loses its grip,
a reminder that three aeroplanes can take me
to her living room but
never her home—

death is a cruel payment
for intimacy, heaven
a jewel, rainforest green
blurred by a mosquito screen

torn by my father's warped vowels,
his slanted English pulls me closer
to myself, wraps me in sandy towels
used on the beaches of Bahia,
a pre-teen me shaded
by coconut trees, the jubilee of colourful
blood splattered on sepia
memories, nostalgia my second most-felt emotion
after *saudades*,
cured briefly by dancing

samba in the dark.

some days
the most Brazilian thing about me is the
mosquito, humming

in my bedroom, i tap my feet along
to its buzz, its bite
the closest thing i have to a family
reunion—

for now, i practice my Portuguese
silently waiting for it
to come in handy,
scouring supermarkets for
a ripe papaya.

MAGICAL	REALISM
black pearl	infested belly
concocted into song	aching in colonized
jubilee of xequerê beads	slur, the seasick
heard in heaven	shipwrecked onto shore
pulse through feathered clouds	and governed by a trade
to be free	of unequal goods

HOLDING HANDS WITH MY GRANDMOTHER

gold links glinting
across my neck reflect
a touch that lives
thirteen thousand
three hundred and
forty-nine
kilometres east

in your wrinkled-map
palms, the ones
that fixed the clasp at my nape,
this assured, yellow metal
that folds with the same bend
as your knuckles and wrists,
interlocked chain
like interlocked hands
like I will never be separated
from you, like

this necklace is long enough
to reach across that
salt mockery
in the middle.

BITTER

ninety-nine percent
cacao

tastes like a broken attempt of
a foreign language

the purest form of
alienation

(give me a whole block of your
finest dark chocolate)

GOING TO CHURCH

it does not have to be a Sunday
for me to feel obliged
to the stained-glass insides,

drawn to the barn when it suits me.
i present me to myself,
forget the wise men,
light myself a candle so

like a lantern,
i glow.

the gospel of my breath echoes,
resounds against tapestry flesh
my glutes, my pews
my head a choir
my heart the altar—

every blink is a prayer.

i have veins of wine
Dionysian shrine,
a belly of purple grapes,
my hair drapes over me
like not what you see in magazines
like not a haircut but the husk
of a coconut defending
creamy blood and tears

of praise, of holy water
of forgive me for
i have not sinned
i've just broken rules that aren't mine
just haven't listened close enough to

my body, also known as
ancient temple
pharaoh's tomb
warm womb
church of worship
not yours to tamper with,
holy trinity, also known as
mind, body, spirit
girl, daughter, sister
sun, moon, stars,
do, not, enter
unless invited.

i was born in church
i will die in one, too.
when i have issues,
i take it up with god.

she listens.

THE FIRST TIME I LEFT

i was a piranha,
demonstrating how to rip
out hearts with silver teeth,

teaching you how to be
the villain
so that the second time,
you could leave me
with ease

and then we repeat,
dragon wrestling
with its own burning tongue,
wondering where the fire
is coming from.

SELF-PORTRAIT OF ME, A LANDSCAPE

sitting inside the purple night,
the moon a pearly fingernail clipping,
i sip on the sap
of an old papaya tree,
a snarling lip
glossy with amber
nursing a toothache

     i am
young and nervous
dreaming of photosynthesis
flirting with the moon's ghost
as it latches onto my eyelids
and blurs into an alcoholic laugh,
sugar-caned and sharp.

the night yawns
waltzing lazily
and i have this superstition
that i am already
     dead
and spirited,
cosmically curious about
what else i can still
attach myself to

OCEAN

an electrical current / to warm my moqueca / from Vovó's kitchen

a chef / to salt my tongue / into Portuguese

a saia azul de Iemanjá / to soak up tears / cried in disguise

in bed, thinking

all of these
repulsive chores
like store-bought monotony

then i eat
then i sleep
then i text you, *i'm bored*
can u send me a picture
of a piranha
so i can look at it

then i cry
at the pharmacy
because it doesn't sell
Band-Aids big enough
for volcanoes
then you reply,
i've been dead
for three years
stop texting me!

insomniac says a prayer

i know i won't
sleep well tonight

i've been drinking
too much caffeine
too much blood
has rushed to my head
and to all three of my hearts

falling asleep is
as easy as moving an
orange tree or
a hive of bees
my thoughts are rooted
and fruitful
sticky and loud
buzzing, beating
screaming of treason

i am a good listener
just not a very
trustworthy one
i spill secrets
the splash waters my garden
including the weeds
now please
please, Senhora, can i sleep?

ETYMOLOGY
after Safia Elhillo

fact: the Portuguese surname *oliveira* translates to *olive tree*
fact: the olive tree is the most praised tree in Greece

if a Portuguese surname upholds a Greek symbol
will the Portuguese man

know his heart as a leaf of peace and offer it to the world
or
become a stranger to the foreign branch lodged in his chest

PURITY (n)

the bible isn't the only place
where you will find the definition for purity,
stamped to the new skin of the serpent's sin

it is in the dictionary
where purity is the   freedom from
immorality   adulteration   contamination
where old french doesn't get any newer
where purity is defined by all the
      vices it avoids, as in
it is only freedom if it is
      a freedom from flaws, as in

there is no such thing as purity.

there is the scientific version
the opposite of pollution
all the   spaces   that haven't been choked
with smoke
the blue patches
      that look more like
      bruises
barely escaping extinction
scientifically speaking
purity is   endangered
      (spoken by the man in the
      thick white lab coat)

then there is the
      quote   native   unquote
identification of it
the one quoted by colonisers, the
      quote   holiness of magical cleanness   unquote

                    the practice of rejecting taboo
                         protecting oneself
                         performing rituals
in primitive thinking
a purity poisoned by outsiders
its own name shape-shifts
into hypocrisy, a self-deprecating joke
that gets told so many times
you can hear it being whispered to
the prison cells

purity is the most misunderstood
victim in the English language

                    boarding a train that is travelling backwards
                         it face-plants into its thick black breath
                    left wondering where all its pearly white went
                              the hairless halo reincarnated
                                   into a de-feathered dove

i want to make something clear:
when i tell you i am pure
what i mean is

my skin is so good at taking compliments from the sun
that when she shines she lingers on me a little longer

the taste of fresh fruit makes me
feel like a strawberry that will never lose her seeds
never not know how to grow

when my ancestors died they carved maps into the stars
each night i read them like gleaming prayers
fill my mind with routes to the good life

when i tell you i am pure
there is nothing missing
there is no rejection
there is no escape
there is no empty space.

when i tell you i am pure
the serpent is pure
too.

CERAMIC CANOPIES

the mosaic of my heartache
is made of shards
from all the good vases
i have dropped,
sealed with my blood
and glazed with transparent promises

i am dying
for a sunset, purple skies cushioned
by cloudy eyes, whose dusk bleeds
orange cordial
staining everything so that even
my grief tastes sweet
and romantic
and i would live
a hundred more lives
beneath these ceramic canopies
for a sugar-rush like this

when the young night's cordial dribbles
through terracotta cracks i catch
it on my tongue,
but the metallic taste of my mistakes
makes me numb

bossa nova

sometimes i think that all this would sound a little better and a little more important if it were set to music but then i remind myself that i'm not a musician even though the beat of my heart sometimes sounds like mozart and then you read your favourite poem of mine out loud and i think, *this is music to my ears, this is art.*

ROOM OF MIRRORS

earth is a room of mirrors	i am a room of mirrors
the pyramids of giza align with orion's belt	my ancestors taught me that light is the greatest guide so i built myself a life that follows the stars,
snakes shed skin like trees shed leaves	like snakes and trees i shed what i no longer need bleeding a volcano ditty,
from earth, the sun and the moon appear the same size	from earth, my heart is the same size as the sun and moon, they have the same unsurvivable heat the same round scars from past encounters it is why i talk to the sky
summer and winter follow persephone's affairs	every winter i crawl back to the underworld barren land, sinning source of heat each summer i emerge into olympus, where my seeds are sown, where all love has grown
every religion knows the word god	and i, like the ancient greeks, like the pharaohs and their tombs, know where to find god— god is an ochre painting on the insides of my eyelids each night she comes to life and paints me dreams to chase
the uterus wears the same dancing shoes as the moon	waxing and waning stepping in cycles, the moon and i have mastered the waltz.
fertile material is found in women and soil	i am a body of fertile soil. creation is the first thing i have in common with the land.

when i look at the wonders of this earth,
all i see is myself.

LIMÃO

in my bowl
of green flesh
oozing and sour
there is sugar from
a land three seas
away, unrefined,
open and unapologetic
to my greed and
my guts and
i have tasted so many
far-away lands
that even i
have become their
fruit, rooted
ripe and cut
up so you can taste
my sour, too

MILK AND OATS

milk and oats
milk and honey
milk will make me lots of money

milk like mother
milk like cream
milk that is spilt makes the counter gleam

LOVE

i am a master
piece when i bleed
i will dip my paintbrush into the
dark red
that is dripping down my leg
and i will paint the word
Love
across my forehead
and i will let go
of the breath i've been holding
for so long
i am the artist and the artwork
you are the observer please
no photographs or harsh
lighting or else the love
might fade

WHAT I KNOW
after Yesika Salgado

1. i will eat Bacalhau à Gomes de Sá for Christmas dinner (cooked by mummy)
2. Lemon Meringue Pie for dessert (Vovó's recipe)
3. how sunlight fixes everything
4. but doesn't bring back the dead
5. the curl of Portuguese around my tongue
6. the strangle of Portuguese words i don't know
7. Scorpio Season
8. my sister's hair
9. my sister's hug
10. thirteen thousand, three hundred and forty-nine kilometres
11. the distance between Sydney and São Paulo
12. if only i were a bird or a fish
13. the luckiest number

INCANTATION

bruna as in
brunette as in
brown hair as in

i fulfilled some sort of prophecy
or
my parents knew of the girl
that this world needed

and named her into existence.

PART II

*i am a ship in the centre
of a continent*

AN OBSERVATION

lined by poplar trees,
hinterland hills of obscene
green fold over
themselves, dirty
jeans fumbling through fields of
porcelain cherubs and emerald energy—

everything is as it's meant to be:

two birds perched
on the spine of a lazy cow
grazing, gazing
at an orchard of overripe
peaches, blushing;

a sweet scene.

that one time mary pranked us

knocked up by that fool gabriel
she knocked back another
saved her marriage, saved face for joseph
claimed gabriel was an angel
claimed an entire religion
just to claim her kid
turned it into a career with hours so long
it lasted two millenniums, a mother so saintly
she got her kid into it, a family business
of con artists we all descend from—
still her daughters hide their miracles
still clip their wings and give them away,
still invent entire religions just so men don't
prey on them, make them pray to them,
towering cathedrals whose underground tombs
hide carcasses of all the secrets
so true they would haunt God
and if there was ever a religion i wanted to follow
it is the one a woman made up.

AN ODE TO THE AUSTRALIAN SUMMER

the first sign of summer is
the echo of cicadas
vibrating against sweaty bellies,
a hasty walk along
hot sand, the mourning
of a white christmas,
a fight over the last ice-block

a hiatus—
no work, no school,
families forced together,
some hoping
or dreading
for it to be over.

as i write this poem,
i realise how much
i do not care for
the australian summer,
how the festivities were borrowed
from winter lands and
born out of place.

i, like christmas,
do not belong.

which is to say

we are a people
who cannot read the signs
in the sand

we are a people

who think the sand
a snow

this isn't really an ode.

it is more of an accusation
of an australian summer
that is too drunk to live up
to its expectations.

RETROGRADE

yesterday when my mother lay
binoculars in my hand
i followed her finger to the full moon

to become an astronomer
i turned off the kitchen light
and undressed the white planet

the craters made it look real
the kitchen smelt of
sweet corn, i should have married you

LADY GAWAIN

i thought of you so i
decapitated myself, my neck
a vase of plucked flowers
my body a volcano cleaning itself
of impurities i thought i could erupt
into a green knight who doesn't
know how to tell apart an axe
from a holly branch
just knows how to hold
her head and ride away
horseback but i still
feel your fingers wrapped around
my spine can someone tell me
how to rip the vertebrae
out of my back and still
ride stubborn into the sunset
limbs and all
trailing behind

PHOTO ALBUM

my heart on film, circa 2002
      a newborn conductor orchestrating her first
      live performance
      strumming heartstrings
      the latest model of a harp
      heartbeat and drum snare
      the audience cries
      the conductor bows

my heart on film, circa 2008
      my first day of school is the first day my heart isn't
      guarded by my mother
      she wraps it in plastic and packs it into my lunchbox
      i don't take it out for the whole day;
      sweaty, the condensation makes the cling wrap
      lose its grip
      a sticky heart loose in my
      unzipped backpack
      the thump of it against my back
      is the soundtrack
      of the next thirteen years of my life

my heart on film, circa 2015
      at the beach, my heart washed up on the shore
      ebbing and flowing
      shards of shell 12mm deep
      in the flesh
      red sea foam like the ocean tried to brush me out of its teeth
      shoving my rejected heart back
      into the gaping hole in my chest
      refusing my gift
      one girl's trash is another girl's treasure
      the ocean seems to only like shiny things.

i tape it back to my chest.

my heart on film, circa 2020
      dressed in healed scars
      it learns, it pours
      out all over white paper
      funnels itself into pens
      ink stains illustrate entire stories
      clawing from the cavity in my chest
      and fastening onto my sleeve
      it bears its teeth for the world to see
      gleaming smile, inky gums.

NOVEMBER

a sympathetic star
casts soft light across
fields of fatigued flowers

forgives winter for its brutality,
summer for its intimacy

swishes the ocean in her mouth
warms it up and waterfalls
into hot springs

she is the space between
      what will
and
      what has

lazy consonants invite weary travellers
to rest by hives of overflowing honey

it is where the road gets
a little sweeter

L90

the bus routes have changed and changed again
the familiar falls short of its destination and
resurrects into another form of home

the seats are still itchy
the windows are scratched with graffiti,
signatures to document
i was here, i was always here

the people in the smoke look grey
look around, look for an empty seat
they never see

this whole continent is under-
populated

dense-less and frothy,
a dry latte ordered with a slack tongue
larttay, larttay,
this coffee-shop hum
of words borrowed and unreturned

but i am here, i was always here
looking out the window
ignoring the itch of my lips
following the bus down the road
through the two-dollar shops
cramped parking spots
yellow-signed stops

this route is my root:
follow it far enough and surely
the soil dampens

GIFTS FROM YOU, BIG BLUE

a three hour
drive to Emily Fuller's
farm,

a vintage dress that fits
just right, blue
sequins and a pocket
of green quartz—

i spotted a koala in the
trees and i knew
the rocks meant
something.

if you're lucky, if you
have green quartz in your pocket,
you go to the beach the next day
and swim for
hours and eat
greasy fish with
your shrivelled fingertips.

the sun on your back
and the murmuring
of farm animals
in the night,
thirty-five degree days
rendering us motion
less, care
less, direction
full.

after swimming
in the dark and swatting
cicadas by campfire
light, i wonder

how much of this
can i fit in my pocket?

FOOD CHAIN

little girl / eaten by her thoughts / eaten by adults / who like interrupting / eaten by retail therapy / lots and lots of retail therapy / consumed by itchy blazers that are four sizes too big but priced at 80% off / eaten by high-brow ideals / like Vogue and espressos / eaten by people who are actually happy / truly happy people / who don't need to drink coffee / to wake up in the morning / eaten by death / eaten by the big fat starry universe / eaten by a worm hole / eaten by a red apple / a very crisp, very shiny red apple / eaten by a little girl.

so there.

SPRINGTIME

three poems ago
i would have written you
into winter,

meandering footprints
through the snow, leading me
off a cliff.

since i wrote myself
into a caterpillar long ago,
my wings unfolded
just in time to save me.

now that i can fly,
you've become an ant.
not even snow is soft enough
for you to tread
across.

you fumble
for the keys to an
empty cocoon.

songs through text

he sent me a song
and then another
and then another
and he said *tell me what you think of this one*
and i listened to it once
and i listened to it again
and i said *i like the song but also*
i don't like the song
and he said *yes i completely*
understand, and then he
said *elaborate*
and i thought, *god*
what is a drum
if it is to always be
skinned so i left
the message
unanswered

and i listened
to a better
song.

MAURICE

i gave maurice my
last two aspirin, my
limbs draped across
furniture on a hot day,
and i say
after they've fizzled in
water they taste
like lemonade.

but i also
sort of needed them
for my
migraine.

now, maurice has a clear
head that gets
wasted on an afternoon
in bed, with a whirring
fan to mock my sweat-
ing body on the living
room floor.

PHARAOH

in ancient Egypt
a priest inserts a metal rod
up a corpse's nose
pulls out the brains
rinses the skull
with alcohol

after that, they remove
all the other
unnecessary
organs like the
lungs and liver and intestines
fish them out like
cheap accessories

leaving the heart
alone
in a corpse
trembling, wondering
how it will
cope all on its own in the afterlife
without a stomach to hold
the butterflies

when i am with you
i feel like
an ancient Egyptian
corpse

you embalm me.

GROCER

i	you
lost	found
all	none
of	of
my	your
money	happiness
trying	trying
to	to
buy	give
all	away
the	the
fruits	fruits
i	you
don't	do
grow	grow

ODE TO 12:30 AM ON A WEDNESDAY (AND ITS SUCCESSOR, 8:15 AM)

sleep is a guest running late.

in her absence,
the moon becomes a lamp
that i count my worries by,
and the unconscious, barefoot
walk to the kitchen is rewarded
with water deeper than the daylight type.

stars tells stories,
secrets turn into oceans
and without sleep to pull me
from the current,
drowning becomes a late-night hobby.

watching me rub sleep
from my eyes,
the sunny Wednesday morning
is guilty of its early intrusion.

it towels me dry.

A DINNER RESERVATION

just like raspberries and fresh cherries
loneliness comes in ripe morsels

be careful not to spill the juice
down the front of your blouse

stains are hard to remove
(but you know that by now)

these days you are a cherry connoisseur
blindfold you and you know their flavour off by heart

solitude is best eaten in small bites
at a table for one
with honey drizzled over the top

an acquired taste.

THE DIVINE ESTATE

a landlady,
brought up a farm girl
trying to be an organic woman

lying on her bed
of flowers, a fever
hot flushed sodden
cotton draped across the valley

cleansed by tears,
a plantation of Muses
growing strong amidst growing pains
playing piano with the bees, honey
seeps from the keys
sticky and groaning
the bees throning
their next Queen.

the drones are patient.
the stingers are sharp.
the pollen is thick.

beneath the cotton
golden rivers run and purple plums grow
ripe and resourceful.

the Queen will never fall
silent, the piano forever resounding
all the way to Venus

where angles hum along, cushioned
by cotton, rotund bellies of plum
swaying, praying

the fever is fleeting
and the Muses are treating
themselves to dessert.

SECOND CHANCES

i just saw this bug and it was walking backwards and i thought what's it doing that for and he kept walking back back back and i thought maybe he lost something and he's retracing his steps or maybe
      this time
he wants to do things the right way.

weeding is a hobby for the lonely

and all this time i thought i'd have you forever / and all this time i forgot how flowers die after they bloom / and i wish i were your petals, dying with you / crying for you / smiling at you / and all this time / goes on / and on / and the flower becomes a bird / of paradise / to pollenate

THE DREADED DINNER PARTY

a slice of lemon in a glass of water
casts kaleidoscopic shards
across a floral tablecloth,
split sunlight slits eyesight
a squint at the roast beef centrepiece,
beetroot juice stains the silverware,
cutlery becomes used weaponry,
the backyard a potential

murder scene,
the culprit wiping down the victim
with a serviette,
too much extra virgin olive oil
dribbling down
a chin, a sip of water, a sour aftertaste,
an announcement for dessert,

a promise for sweetness bound to be broken:
lemon tart. no meringue. dirty forks.
a pause while the guests pray
that they don't need to wash the dishes.
a bite of tart. a sip of water. a bitter affair.
flies hover around
neglected crumbs, guests swat
smiling, eyes glazed over,
a sugary film just sweet enough
to cover the uncooked curd.

Vovó, eu esto
esperando você
na cozinha.

DARLING,

if i could introduce myself
a second time, i wouldn't
at all. i would steer clear
from your clippers

my stomach of black pearls
will be left unscooped
untouched

don't you know?
these orange cheeks
do a lot more than
hold your kisses

if i could introduce myself
a second time, a second time,
i wouldn't at all.
i would be the world's
biggest secret

i would spread
rumours like the white flowers
of a lime tree
too delicate to pick,
proof of a citrus heart
not loved enough
for lemonade

so next time you find my seeds,
Darling,
plant them for me.

anonymous

missing u again. wondering if i can let u know telepathically. as if i forgot that our souls are tethered historically, not cosmically. hoping u receive this message, hoping u don't. hoping u feel this ache, too.

PART III

*this ocean kisses
distant shores*

AN ORIGIN STORY

I.
under coconut trees
my grandmother's silver perm
reflected in my grandfather's aviators
and behind them
an entire ocean filled with sugar
thick as condensed
milk

II.
onto the brazilian moon
the silhouettes of my grandparents
flicker, my father reflected
in silver hair and metal rims
the moon bends into a crescent
sweet smile

III.
inside my grandmother's kitchen,
a family of faces reflects off
pearly plates licked clean
the vow of a coconut dessert
makes me wonder
how it could get any sweeter
than this

SÃO PAULO

city of concrete monuments
sky of helicopter pads
handbag shops to follow my mother into
Havaiana market to follow my father into
follow father like soldier follows shield
cafes of kibe, always good kibe
Ibirapuera park
of coconut vendors
of sweaty joggers
of architecture so dramatic
i finally realise it is an art
just to walk past

WALKING   DEAD

treading soil	a burial beneath
sown with seeds	of bodies
to sprout	memories decomposed
to travel	into a legacy
like floating coconut	on a shore unbound
by bottomless ocean	by the next life
upon holy saltwater	unhusked and ungraved
this poem walks	again and awake

THIEVES OF IGUAÇU

robbing a Portuguese shipwreck,
i use every chest of
16th century gold
to bribe the ferryman
for a paddle up
the Iguaçu Falls where angel
wings are easily
mistaken for mist

each time he refuses,
i am left to stare
at millions of my
decaying reflections, each
with the familiar seaweed scent
of being lost for so long,
each sobbing prayers
for your return,
sinking canoes with
seasick tears

if i let the waterfall
drag me into its bowels,
will you fly down
to resurrect me?

or will i be faced
by the ferryman
bearing a mob of slaves
whose gold has no place
in the hands of
this desperate girl who
through her serpentine history
in nature's heights

at death's doorstep
searches for you.

robbed by the afterlife

i refill my room with
the salvaged treasures   of your rising ship.

PRESERVED

curl of hand over mango
wet of pulp beneath jewellery
bowl of mangos never empty
lime juice squeezed over flesh
      drawing me
         to immortality

SAINT DIVA

Senhora,
you are an ancient myth
of a god whose opulent shrine
is wedged into my ribcage,
glowing royal purple
and suspended
by angel wings,

i rise to you

plunging my fist
into my chest
to offer candlelight,
hoping you will take it
and whisper it
into a star
like you did
so glamorously to yourself,
the sky a map of your wisdom

to which when i look up,
i mumble prayers thinking
you will mistake them
for your own heartbeat
and hum along, reminiscent of
a samba song that brings you
dancing from your grave,
satin heels gliding
across latin oceans,
swaying—

even in the dark,
your golden heart

gleams, Holy Treasure,
priceless artefact
beholding all the
powers of gravity yet
weightlessly levitating

under skies alight with your love,
i find my purpose.

ANATOMY OF
THE HAND OF VOVÓ
after Karla Cordero

wrist:	riverbed of purple ancestry
heel:	cheek of papaya flesh overripe
palm:	cut-glass chalice collects pulp
finger:	macaw claw to take off, to land
knuckle:	mound of earth to hold seedling
fingernail:	machete slices guava rind. swift.

CENOURA E CEBOLA

i have walked up and down
Jordanópolis remembering
the Portuguese words for
    carrot and onion
knowing one
from the other
like proud
    proof of citizenship
like if repeating them enough
would sow me into their soil

i have walked up and down
Vovó's kitchen remembering
the Brazilian recipe for
    brigadeiros
recipe like prayer
creation like initiation
chocolate truffle prophecies
take a third eye to come true, like if
    i take them
to a different kitchen
different country
i can keep another's tongue

i have walked up and down
my bedroom remembering
where i left
    myself, the soil
beneath yesterday's vegetable stalls
Vovó's memories of my young Portuguese
the paperless recipe
lying on my desk
that is paperless, too,

      over there
where i left

where i know i can find myself
     in pantries
      on tablecloths
under some other sun that doesn't
burn everything it touches

and now i can't find my grandmother
to congratulate me for remembering

     a place is no good
     if it does not remind you
     of who you are

POCKET-MAP

Vovó's fingers
are soursop-flesh directories
in the fruit aisle

Mamãe's wrists
pave pink guides
to my guava bloodline

My daughter's unborn fist
salutes passionfruit vines
of my destination

My palms lined with these
road-maps, roots deep,
fit perfectly in my pocket.

A 37-DEGREE DAY AT THE FEIRA

it is too sticky to enjoy a papaya,
the Brazilian air challenging me
against my own self—

can i eat a juicy papaya
and let the heat congeal pulp on my chin
use my wrists as serviettes
a buzzing feira becoming a fruity mess
or will i save it for a cooler day
a less Brazilian one
as if identity is measured in degrees celsius
and adjusted with an accent
pulp stuck between teeth like evidence

as if the Australian me can't handle the
juice stains on the Brazilian me

whether i am Brazilian or Australian should not be
a decision to be made
or a meal on a 37-degree day at the feira.

i like my papaya best
in Vovó's kitchen
dripping in lime juice
with a fork and
guardanapo.

i do not have to use my wrists
to know that
i am Brazilian.

NECTAR

the more i am eaten by mosquitos,
the more i am sure my blood is sweet.

if the amazon rainforest is the lungs of the earth, then somewhere in there is the heart

salivating, a fluorescent-yellow
man sees the trees
hoists his knife
and fork and feasts

on my medium-rare
heart, trees
fall around us
the air tastes metallic
cutlery dripping with
blood and
sap and
if only i could plant a
forest in the gaping hole
of my chest

hearts
like leafy greens
are easily chewed

the chainsaw's
scream drowns out
my own, a ruined
land is a
heartless one.

SYNONYMS FOR LIGHT

something to be found / in every sky / as três marias / like lamp over ocean / like secret message over border / morse code / the smile of my family on FaceTime / the yellow of their distant kitchen / illuminated by glowing oven / the glint of their forks / the glint of my knives / Vovó's eyes are a torch / searching beneath soil / the end of a tunnel / the end of a life / a candle at the altar / flickering by her breath / the click of a gas stove / the meal it cooks / the family it collects

BRUNA

like an exotic fruit,
people taste my name and ask,
where is that from?
to some, it is so unfamiliar
that they cannot pronounce it right,
and after being corrected,
they give up the name entirely

and call me *B*
as if my name is theirs to
amputate,
as if *Bruna* is a mouthful of
more than you can chew,
and not an
entire story.

after tasting the fruit some more,
rolling it around their mouths,
catching juice down their chin,
they spit it out.

i come from a legacy of rejected fruits:
my sister's name gets its vowels replaced
over and over
until the fruit has been genetically
modified, seedless
and easy to digest.
my father's name gets
introduced to substitutes,
a basket of fruit that contains all
but his own.

these days, when asked my name,
i catch myself
saying something other
than *Bruna*.
i am too afraid that
nobody is ready
to hear a
story
in reply.

to claim my power would be
to claim myself

    Bruna

the whole story.

BRIGADEIRO RECIPE

in saucepan on low heat melt butter. add condensed milk. add cocoa powder. stir until elastic bubbles stretch wide enough to seal a heart. keep stirring, arm aching. labour of love. stop when you tilt the pan and the mixture comes clean off the bottom. like time has made it so thick it has a life of its own. as if heat turned the ingredients into a lifelong bond of family who go everywhere together. turn off heat. let it cool. roll balls of mixture between palms, making globes of chocolate with fingers slightly damp. new earths for new lives. bite size. to be eaten in one country and transported to another. coat in chocolate sprinkles. rest in small paper liners (my favourite are the ones with the copacabana pattern). feed family. feed history. feed home.

HOW TO SAY "I LOVE YOU"

Every night, mummy calls grandma and asks about her day. On Sundays, my sister bakes cookies that will last the week. In the mornings, daddy drives me to work. Even when it's not on his way. When i don't show up to school, my friend texts, *everything ok? x* Five years after her death, i found a letter from Vovó saying how much she misses me. A home-cooked meal. A reminder. "When I saw this I thought of you…"

EVERYONE DIES

the first sign of losing you
was my father's muffled tears

salty stains i cannot scrub
from my memories

the second sign was the flashbacks
screaming all the things
i could have done
to savour you,
edit my negligence out of the draft

and then there was all
the empty spaces:
the abandoned kitchen
yellow and echoing
the birthday cards without your loopy scrawl
un-bought at the gift store
the country whose trees have lost their fruit
soil turned rotten
the part of my brain i leave vacant

                                  the part of my brain i occupy
                                  fruits crawl back to roots
                                        and ripen, multiply
                              to feed five thousand days more

                        where my birthday cards bear three stamps
                and a return address written in your loopy scrawl
                          proof that my birthday exists there, too

      where a green kitchen bathes in a home-baked aroma,
            sings to the shuffling of your slippers,
            sets out an extra plate for a far-away me

                    and the story is published with
                              a happy ending,
                      flash-forward to what it
                could have would have been—
                    my memories are not tear
                                    ful
                    my father is not mother
                                less

                  and no one ever really dies

TESOURO
after Yesika Salgado

a papaya tree
has fed a thousand generations
of women
in one sitting;
a family gathering defies
mortality, hearts
have a place at the table
without a body to hold them,
hanging from branches,
glistening rubies, bejewelled
women share
stories like recipes,
secretive and proud.

if my Vovó's kitchen is
the centre of the universe,
then our stories are the
gravity that keeps us
connected,
bowls of ripe fruit are
chests of Tesouro,
proof that we are rich
with love, a bewitching
display of what it means to be
daughter
granddaughter
sister
girl
woman.

there are many ways to be
me, all of which

are safe
beneath the shade
of a papaya tree.

TUCANO IN THE SKY

driving down highway from campos do jordão to ilhabela. from pinching cold to mosquito bite. car winds around mountains. big truck of yogurt ahead and green rainforest behind. and i spot a tucano in the sky. beak so colourful i though Frida had mistaken brazil for a canvas. feather chest puffed with pride. flapping towards the ocean. and the best thing i can tell you is that none of this is made up. i saw a tucano in the sky.

GOMES

To my papai,
the first to give me a nickname
longer than my real name,
long enough to reach across
the sea and hold onto the roots
of our family tree,
Papai, who gives advice
with the same pride
he had tying my shoelaces,
a pride of saving me from falling,
a pride of knowing he fell a thousand times before me,
my father gives advice
long enough to reach back in time
to his mistakes and show them how to do it
the right way.

To my mummy,
whose hands have caught so many of my tears
that they smell of seaweed,
cupping my oceans in her seabed palms
offering me my own reflection,
my mummy has been to six continents,
has travelled the world and witnessed
almost every type of magic,
when she speaks of her journeys i realise
these tidal waves
that keep me tied
are only her hands
turning water into home.

To my sister,
shape-shifter, mermaid
summoned two and a half years after me

to teach me how to follow in someone's footsteps
without wearing their shoes,
her tears are made of healing water,
the same stuff as the sea
she shows me
the secret ingredient of sisterhood
that i drink by the jar,
my irmã shakes the world
like a snow-globe
she is why my head is filled with glitter.

To my tios,
who prepare for my arrival like Christmas,
who keep an extra set of sheets
for my sister and me, always ready to let us rest
who let us clumsily strum their guitars
steal their brigadeiros
ask the unanswerable questions,
the questions they don't have enough English for,
the questions i store for years in my throat
just to serve alongside the churrasco.
next time i'm there, let's turn the questions and guitars
into a song, when i'm gone
we can sing along to each other's curiosity.

To my tia,
who is mine not by blood but by love,
whose perfume hugs me before her arms arrive,
who has survived cancer, not just her own
but her mother's and brother's,
has looked death in the eye
dared it to a dance battle
just to prove that she is not his dance floor
my tia knows how to make me feel pretty,
knows when a xicara de cha will stitch me back up,

knows how to say "I love you"
without making it a familial obligation,
an "I love you" so believable that i know
how love exists without blood.

To my Vovó,
who lives in so many of my poems
that now i write just to make sure she still has a home,
Vovó could make friends with anyone
even the German tourists she met four seconds before,
her friendship so powerful
that it reaches me from the afterlife,
a shaft of sunlight through muddy clouds,
Vovó knew her way around the morning feira
as if she'd built each stall from the ground up,
as if she'd planted the papaya trees
just so she could shop for them
with her granddaughters trailing behind,
as if she knew that someday she'd have to show
little girls how to go make a life of their own
my Vovó brought heaven to earth
she is the reason i see so many angels.

To my family.
there is nothing more i want to
      be
      belong to
      be there for
than you.

Acknowledgements

This book of poetry was inspired by my family's love and stories, for which I am forever grateful. Mummy, Daddy, Milena, Kadu, Piti, Karina, Grandma, and Diane, thank you all, obrigada.

Thank you to my teacher and friend, Alison Roberts, who not only helped me edit this book, but inspired the confidence in me to create this book.

Thank you to all my friends who get excited with me about my poems' stories—thank you Lara for your everlasting ruminations and conceptualisations, thank you Emily for your ecstatic devotion to nature, thank you Olivia for your determination to read everything I've written.

Of course, thank you to Cynthia Brackett-Vincent, Eddie Vincent, Deirdre Wait, and the wonderful Encircle family who continue to turn my dreams into a reality. I feel so lucky to have your support.

Finalmente, obrigada Vovó.

Previous Publications

Thank you to the poetry journals in which my poems have previously appeared:
"Brasileira" (*Mosman Council*, October 2020)
"if the amazon rainforest is the lungs of the earth, then somewhere in there is the heart" (*The Pangolin Review*, April 2021)
"that one time mary pranked us," "Going to Church," "Pharaoh" (*Dodging the Rain*, April 2021)
"Food Chain" (*Cacti Fur*, October 2021)
"Etymology" (*Cordite Poetry Review*, October 2021).

About the Author

Bruna Gomes is an Australian-Brazilian novelist and poet. Her writing plants cultural and emotional history with new seeds. In 2021, at eighteen years of age, she published her debut novel *How to Disappear* with Encircle Publications, and her work is featured in numerous online journals. She has received awards in various Sydney-based writing competitions, including the 2020 Mosman Youth Awards in Literature. Bruna was born in Boston, Massachusetts, and grew up on the Northern Beaches of Sydney, Australia. When she's not writing, she enjoys eating almond croissants and reading at the beach.

If you enjoyed reading this book,
please consider writing your honest review
and sharing it with other readers.

Many of our Authors are happy to participate in
Book Club and Reader Group discussions.
For more information, contact us at info@encirclepub.com.

Thank you,
Encircle Publications

For news about more exciting new poetry, join us at:

Facebook: www.facebook.com/encirclepub

Instagram: www.instagram.com/encirclepublications

Twitter: twitter.com/encirclepub

Sign up for Encircle Publications newsletter and specials:
eepurl.com/cs8taP

www.ingramcontent.com/pod-product-compliance
Lightning Source LLC
Chambersburg PA
CBHW060406080526
44583CB00012B/484